For

For My Mom
Copyright © 1993
Peter Pauper Press, Inc.
202 Mamaroneck Avenue
White Plains, NY 10601
All rights reserved
ISBN 0-88088-135-6
Printed in Hong Kong
7   6   5   4   3

Introduction

Roses, the most beautiful of all flowers, have fascinated people for thousands of years (and even existed in prehistoric times, as shown by fossil remains of leaves and thorns).

Greek philosophers and poets mention many different varieties of roses. During Roman times roses were used in daily life—given to loved ones as gifts, fashioned into wreaths for guests at celebrations, and spread over tombs to honor the departed. The petals were used to make a tart, a wine, and rose oil for medicinal purposes.

Roses continued to increase in popularity as many new varieties were developed. Today there are thousands!

The rose has come to symbolize beauty, romance, love, and fragrance. Bouquets and corsages are given to celebrate milestones like weddings, birthdays, and anniversaries. Perhaps you fondly remember an occasion when you received these special flowers, and how they made you feel. Even without words, a dozen roses can say "I love you."

No other flower has received more poetic tributes. From the Bible to Shakespeare, to more recent times, roses have been celebrated in poetry and prose—as we shall see!

E. L. B.

Reign endless, Rose!
for fair you are,
Nor heaven reserves
a fairer thing.
HERMAN MELVILLE

What's in a name? That which
we call a rose
By any other name would smell
as sweet.

WILLIAM SHAKESPEARE,
Romeo and Juliet

*T*his is the way, walk ye in it. The wilderness and the solitary place shall be glad for them; and the desert shall rejoice, and blossom as the rose.

ISAIAH 35:1

*A*nd she was fair as is
the rose in May.

GEOFFREY CHAUCER,
Legend of Cleopatra

*S*he wore a wreath of roses,
The night that first we met.

THOMAS HAYNES BAYLY,
She Wore a Wreath of Roses

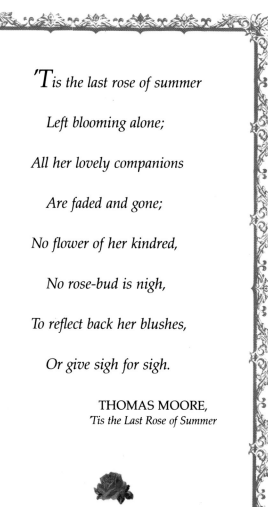

'Tis the last rose of summer

Left blooming alone;

All her lovely companions

Are faded and gone;

No flower of her kindred,

No rose-bud is nigh,

To reflect back her blushes,

Or give sigh for sigh.

THOMAS MOORE,
'Tis the Last Rose of Summer

I'd rather have roses on my table than diamonds on my neck.

EMMA GOLDMAN

He who would have beautiful Roses in his garden must have beautiful Roses in his heart.

DEAN HOLE

Here's to friendship, the only rose without thorns!

TOAST

The sweetest flower that blows,
  I give you as we part
For you it is a rose
    For me it is my heart.

FREDERICK PETERSON,
At Parting

Go pretty rose, go to my fair,
Go tell her all I fain would dare,
Tell her of hope; tell her of spring,
Tell her of all I fain would sing,
Oh! were I like thee, so fair a thing.

MIKE BEVERLY,
Go Pretty Rose

The rose was awake all night
  for your sake,
Knowing your promise to me;
The lilies and roses were all awake,
They sighed for the dawn and thee.

ALFRED, LORD TENNYSON,
Maud

Like the rose, Mighty like the rose, A rose is a rose is an onion.

ERNEST HEMINGWAY,
For Whom the Bell Tolls

Rose is a rose is a rose is a rose.

GERTRUDE STEIN,
Sacred Emily

Live now, believe me, wait not till tomorrow.
Gather the roses of life today.

PIERRE DE RONSARD,
Sonnets pour Hélène

Roses have thorns, and silver
  fountains mud;
Clouds and eclipses stain both
  moon and sun,
And loathsome canker lives in sweetest
  bud.
All men make faults.

WILLIAM SHAKESPEARE,
Sonnet 35

Ring around the rosie,
A pocket full of posies
Ashes, ashes
All fall down.

CHILDREN'S RHYME

Growing old is no cause for hysteria. The
rose bush does not scream when the petals
begin to fall.

DOUGLAS MEADOR

What though youth gave love
  and roses,
Age still leaves us friends and wine.

THOMAS MOORE,
Spring and Autumn

Gather therefore the rose, whilst yet
  is prime,
For soon comes age, that will her pride
  deflower.

EDMUND SPENSER,
The Faerie Queene

Won't you come into the garden? I would like my roses to see you.

ROSE HENNIKER HESTON,
The Perfect Hostess

Don't strew me with roses after
I'm dead.
When Death claims the light of
my brow,
No flowers of life will cheer me: instead
You may give me my roses now!

THOMAS F. HEALEY,
Give Me My Roses Now

I took her for a rose, but she breedeth a burr.

JOHN HEYWOOD,
Proverbs

There is nothing more difficult for a truly creative painter than to paint a rose, because before he can do so he has first to forget all the roses that were ever painted.

HENRI MATISSE

*T*was a yellow rose,
By that south window of the little house,
My cousin Romney gathered with his
hand
On all my birthdays, for me, save the
last;
And then I shook the tree too rough,
too rough
For roses to stay after.

ELIZABETH BARRETT BROWNING,
Aurora Leigh

*H*e came and took me by the hand,
  Up to a red rose tree,
He kept His meaning to Himself,
  But gave a rose to me.

I did not pray Him to lay bare
  The mystery to me,
Enough the rose was Heaven to smell,
  And His own face to see.

RALPH HODGSON,
The Mystery

I watched a rose-bud very long
  Brought on by dew and sun and
    shower,
  Waiting to see the perfect flower:
Then when I thought it should be strong
  It opened at the matin hour
And fell at even-song.

CHRISTINA G. ROSSETTI,
Symbols

*H*ow *fair is the Rose! What a beautiful*
flower.
  The glory of April and May!
But the leaves are beginning to fade
in an hour,
  And they wither and die in a day.
Yet the Rose has one powerful virtue to
boast,
  Above all the flowers of the field;
When its leaves are all dead, and fine
colors are lost,
  Still how sweet a perfume it will yield!

ISAAC WATTS,
The Rose

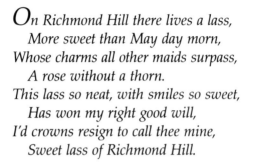

On Richmond Hill there lives a lass,
  More sweet than May day morn,
Whose charms all other maids surpass,
  A rose without a thorn.
This lass so neat, with smiles so sweet,
  Has won my right good will,
I'd crowns resign to call thee mine,
  Sweet lass of Richmond Hill.

LEONARD MacNALLY,
The Lass of Richmond Hill

*God made Himself an awful rose
of dawn.*

ALFRED, LORD TENNYSON,
The Vision of Sin

*Oh roses for the flush of youth,
And laurel for the perfect prime;
But pluck an ivy branch for me
Grown old before my time.*

CHRISTINA G. ROSSETTI,
Song

*At Christmas I no more desire a rose
Than wish a snow in May's new-
     fangled mirth.*

WILLIAM SHAKESPEARE,
Love's Labor's Lost

*Someone said that God gave us memory
so that we might have roses in December.*

JAMES M. BARRIE

Treaties, you see, are like girls and roses:
they last while they last.

CHARLES DE GAULLE

The growth of a large business is merely
a survival of the fittest. . . . The American
beauty rose can be produced in the
splendor and fragrance which bring cheer
to its beholder only by sacrificing the early
buds which grow up around it.

JOHN D. ROCKEFELLER

The fairest things have fleetest end,
Their scent survives their close:
But the rose's scent is bitterness
To him that loved the rose.

FRANCIS THOMPSON,
Daisy

*A*ny nose
May ravage with impunity a rose.

ROBERT BROWNING,
Sordello

*H*e wears the rose
Of youth upon him.

WILLIAM SHAKESPEARE,
Antony and Cleopatra

A rose is sweeter in the bud than
full-blown.

JOHN LYLY,
Euphues and His England

*I*t is the month of June,
    The month of leaves and roses,
When pleasant sights salute the eyes,
    And pleasant scents the noses.

N. P. WILLIS,
The Month of June

Roses red and violets blue,
And all the sweetest flowers that in
the forest grew.

EDMUND SPENSER,
The Faerie Queene

Rose of the Garden! such is woman's
lot—
Worshipp'd while blooming—when
she fades, forgot.

THOMAS MOORE,
Rose of the Desert

From fairest creatures we desire
increase,
That thereby beauty's rose might
never die.

WILLIAM SHAKESPEARE,
Sonnet 1

We all love a pretty girl—under
the rose.

ISAAC BICKERSTAFFE,
Love in a Village

Loveliest of lovely things are they
On earth that soonest pass away.
The rose that lives its little hour
Is prized beyond the sculptured flower.

WILLIAM CULLEN BRYANT,
A Scene on the Banks of the Hudson

A rose to the living is more
Than sumptuous wreaths to the dead.

NIXON WATERMAN,
A Rose to the Living

It was not in the winter
Our loving lot was cast!
It was the time of roses,
We plucked them as we passed!

THOMAS HOOD,
It Was Not in the Winter

*And I wove the thing to a random
   rhyme,*
*For the Rose is Beauty, the Gardener,
   Time.*

AUSTIN DOBSON,
A Fancy from Fontenelle

The bride hath paced into the hall,
Red as a rose is she.

SAMUEL TAYLOR COLERIDGE,
The Ancient Mariner

*Alas, that Spring should vanish with
   the Rose!*
*That Youth's sweet-scented Manuscript
   should close!*

EDWARD FITZGERALD

With rue my heart is laden
For golden friends I had,
For many a rose-lipt maiden
And many a lightfoot lad.

By brooks too broad for leaping
The lightfoot boys are laid;
The rose-lipt girls are sleeping
In fields where roses fade.

A. E. HOUSMAN,
A Shropshire Lad

How splendid in the morning glows
    the lily; with what grace he throws
His supplication to the rose.

JAMES ELROY FLECKER,
Golden Journey to Samarkand

If love were what the rose is,
And I were like the leaf,
Our lives would grow together
In sad or singing weather.

ALGERNON C. SWINBURNE,
A Match

But earthlier happy is the rose distill'd,
Than that which withering on the virgin thorn
Grows, lives, and dies, in single blessedness.

WILLIAM SHAKESPEARE,
A Midsummer Night's Dream

The rose has thorns only for those who would pluck it.

CHINESE PROVERB

I seek a form that my style cannot discover, a bud of thought that wants to be a rose.

RUBEN DARIO,
I Seek a Form

Sweet spring, full of sweet days and roses,
A box where sweets compacted lie.

GEORGE HERBERT,
The Temple

Come into the garden, Maud,
  For the black bat, night, has flown;
Come into the garden, Maud,
  I am here at the gate alone;
And the woodbine spices are wafted
abroad,
    And the musk of the rose is blown.
                    ALFRED, LORD TENNYSON,
                              Maud

A rosebud set with little wilful thorns,
And sweet as English air could make
    her, she.
                    ALFRED, LORD TENNYSON,
                              The Princess

He who wants a rose must respect the
thorn.

                    PERSIAN PROVERB

A rose too often smelled loses its fragrance.
SPANISH PROVERB

*H*e that plants thorns must never expect to gather roses.

PILPAY

*B*ecause the rose must fade,
Shall I not love the rose?
RICHARD WATSON GILDER

*I*f folks will let the roses alone, the thorns will let them be.
T. C. HALIBURTON (SAM SLICK),
Wise Saws

Rose-Scented Potpourri

½   cup rose buds or rose petals
1½ cups old-fashioned rose geranium
1½ cups true rose geranium
½   teaspoon ground cloves

Home-grown roses and most wild roses have plentiful fragrance while many florist roses lack the beloved rose scent. If gathering rosebuds, pick them after dew or rain has evaporated. Pick the petals of open flowers before they fade and when dry, also.

Rose buds, because of their thickness, need to dry thoroughly, and be stored separately from petals.

The clove spice is optional; it adds an indescribable depth to the rose scent as well as increases the longevity of the fragrance.

The roses of pleasure seldom last long enough to adorn the brow of him who plucks them; for they are the only roses which do not retain their sweetness after they have lost their beauty.

HANNAH MORE

An idealist is one who, on noticing that a rose smells better than a cabbage, concludes that it will also make better soup.

H. L. MENCKEN

Sweet as the rose that died last year is the rose that is born today.

COSMO MONKHOUSE,
A Dead March

Roses at first were white,

Till they co'd not agree

Whether my Sappho's breast,

Or they more white sho'd be.

But being vanquisht quite,

A blush their cheeks bespread,

Since which (believe the rest)

The Roses first came red.

ROBERT HERRICK,
How Roses Came Red

I sent my love two roses—one
    As white as driven snow,
And one a blushing royal red,
    A flaming Jacqueminot.

My heart sank when I met her: sure
    I had been overbold,
For on her breast my pale rose lay
    In virgin whiteness cold.

Yet with low words she greeted me,
    With smiles divinely tender;
Upon her cheek the red rose dawned—
    The white rose meant surrender.

JOHN HAY,
The White Flag

Herbal Love Bath

Ingredients:

1	cup lavender
1	cup rosemary
1	cup rose petals
½	cup rose geranium leaves
½	cup lemon verbena leaves
1	tablespoon each thyme, mint, sage, and orrisroot powder

Method:

Combine all ingredients. Mix thoroughly and keep in a tightly lidded container. To make a bath ball, pack ¼ cup in a muslin square and tie securely. Bring to a boil in 1 cup of water and let stand for 10 minutes. Add the bath ball to hot bath water and use it to scrub yourself. Relax in the bath and let your thoughts focus on romance.

Each Morn a thousand Roses brings,
* you say;*
Yes, but where leaves the Rose of
* Yesterday?*
THE RUBAIYAT OF OMAR KHAYYAM

A rose is fairest when 'tis budding new,
And hope is brightest when it dawns from fears;
And rose is sweetest washed with morning dew,
And love is loveliest when embalmed in tears.

SIR WALTER SCOTT,
The Lady of the Lake

To gather life's roses, unscathed by the briar.

WALTER SCOTT,
Ivanhoe

Two roses on one slender spray
  In sweet communion grew,
Together hailed the morning ray
  And drank the evening dew.

MONTGOMERY,
The Roses